MW01701623

AMERICAN HERO

BY **BESS WOHL**

★

★

DRAMATISTS
PLAY SERVICE
INC.

AMERICAN HERO
Copyright © 2014, Bess Wohl

SPECIAL NOTE

Anyone receiving permission to produce AMERICAN HERO is required to give credit to the Author(s) as sole and exclusive Author(s) of the Play on the title page of all programs distributed in connection with performances of the Play and in all instances in which the title of the Play appears, including printed or digital materials for advertising, publicizing or otherwise exploiting the Play and/or a production thereof. Please see your production license for font size and typeface requirements.

Be advised that there may be additional credits required in all programs and promotional material. Such language will be listed under the "Additional Billing" section of production licenses. It is the licensee's responsibility to ensure any and all required billing is included in the requisite places, per the terms of the license.

SPECIAL NOTE ON SONGS AND RECORDINGS

For performances of copyrighted songs, arrangements or recordings mentioned in these Plays, the permission of the copyright owner(s) must be obtained. Other songs, arrangements or recordings may be substituted provided permission from the copyright owner(s) of such songs, arrangements or recordings is obtained; or songs, arrangements or recordings in the public domain may be substituted.

For the sandwich artists

The world premiere of AMERICAN HERO was produced by the Williamstown Theatre Festival (Jenny Gersten, Artistic Director) during its 2013 season. It was directed by Leigh Silverman; the scenic design was by Timothy R. Mackabee; the costume design was by Clint Ramos; the lighting design was by Jennifer Schriever; and the sound design was by Jill BC Du Boff. The cast was as follows:

SHERI .... Erin Wilhelmi
TED .... James Waterston
JAMIE .... Ari Graynor
BOB/CUSTOMER/
SANDWICH/GREGORY .... Omar Metwally

The New York premiere of AMERICAN HERO was produced by Second Stage Theatre (Carole Rothman, Artistic Director; Casey Reitz, Executive Director) in May 2014. It was directed by Leigh Silverman; the set design was by Dane Laffrey; the costume design was by Clint Ramos; the lighting design was by Jennifer Schriever; the sound design was by Jill BC Du Boff; and the production stage manager was Stephen Milosevich. The cast was as follows:

SHERI .... Erin Wilhelmi
TED .... Jerry O'Connell
JAMIE .... Ari Graynor
BOB/CUSTOMER/
SANDWICH/GREGORY .... Daoud Heidami

CHARACTERS

SHERI: 18. Awkward, soft-spoken, and weird. Doesn't stand up straight, ever. Utterly exhausted.

TED: 40ish. Relentlessly positive. A follower of rules. A true believer in the American Dream. Secretly in despair.

JAMIE: 30ish. Hot. Gum snapping. Sexy mini-skirts. Glittery eye shadow. Full of rage.

BOB: 40s. New to America. Thick, unplaceable accent. Very anxious for unknown reasons.

CUSTOMER: 40s. A regular guy who wants a sandwich.

SANDWICH: 40s. A sandwich.

GREGORY: 40s. A man from corporate.

PLACE

A toasted subs franchise somewhere in America.

Tables, chairs, and a sandwich counter.

NOTE

When a double slash (//) appears, it denotes overlapping dialogue. The next line should begin at the double slash, over the line that is being spoken.

"Quiznos has killed me. Destroyed my life. Destroyed my family life for the past seven years. It has been a harrowing experience. Can someone stop this? … I believe there will be justice. But it will be too late for me."

— From the suicide note of
Bhupinder Baber, Quiznos franchisee,
who walked into his Quiznos on Nov. 27, 2007
and shot himself in the chest three times.

AMERICAN HERO

Scene 1

An empty storefront in a strip mall. Sheri sits at a small table opposite Bob, who is reading from a large manual with some difficulty.

BOB. … For Grand Opening. Manager and franchise owner. *(Looks up.)* That is me. Bob. *(Looks back down.)* Will hire three sandwich artists. *(Looks back up.)* That is you.
SHERI. *(Introducing herself.)* Sheri.
BOB. Okay. *(He looks back down, finding his place.)* To be considered, applicant must fill out job application form. *(He finds a form and passes it to her.)*
SHERI. Okay. *(She spends a while filling it out. Bob watches her carefully. She looks up at him periodically, quite uncomfortable. She finishes and reads it over one last time.)* I think I'm done. *(He holds his hand out. She passes him the form. He scans it.)*
BOB. This is "i"?
SHERI. Yeah. Sheri with an "i." *(A pause. He frowns. Shakes his head. Sheri slumps in her seat, without hope. She picks at a hang nail. At long last, he looks up at her. He sighs.)*
BOB. You are hired. *(Sheri perks up.)*
SHERI. Cool. *(Sheri tries to sit up a tiny bit straighter. Bob looks troubled.)*

Scene 2

The store is still mostly empty, but a few more lights are operational and a sandwich counter has been installed.

Several new tables and chairs have appeared. Stools are stacked in a corner. A Coke machine sits on a counter, not yet hooked up.

Bob addresses Sheri, along with two other new employees, Ted and Jamie. He reads from his manual. Ted is taking notes. Jamie is twitchy and restless. Sheri is falling asleep.

BOB. *(Reading.)* The jobs are baser. Finisher. Wrapper. *(To Sheri.)* You shall be baser. *(To Jamie.)* You shall be finisher. *(To Ted.)* You shall be wrapper. *(Thinks, then again to Ted.)* No, you shall be finisher. *(To Jamie.)* You shall be wrapper. No, you shall be baser. No. Hmmm. *(To Ted.)* You shall be finisher. *(To Jamie.)* You shall be wrapper. *(Decided now.)* Baser. Finisher. Wrapper. I am manager. *(Happy with this, he goes back to reading.)* First. Baser. You shall introduce the sandwich. Questions you must ask are, "For here or to go?" "White or wheat or wrap or multigrain flatbread?" Or, "Would you like 'enter condiments here'?" *(Looking up.)* Try.
SHERI. *(Waking up.)* What?
BOB. Try! The questions! "For here, or … "
SHERI. For here or …
BOB. To go!
SHERI. To go.
BOB. Keep going.
SHERI. Um, what was the next question —
BOB. White or wheat or wrap or multigrain flatbread.
SHERI. White … Or wheat … Or wrap or …
BOB. Or multigrain flatbread!
SHERI. Multigrain flatbread.
BOB. Would you like, "Enter condiments here."
SHERI. Would you like, "Enter condiments here." *(He stares at her in disbelief.)*

BOB. Enter a condiment.
SHERI. What?
BOB. Enter a condiment!
SHERI. How?
BOB. "Enter a condiment here."
SHERI. Um …
JAMIE. *(At last, exploding with irritation.)* Honey mustard.
BOB. *(To Jamie.)* Are *you* baser?
JAMIE. No.
BOB. That's what I thought. *(Turns back to Sheri.)* Baser.
SHERI. Honey mustard.
BOB. Very good. Now. Finisher.
TED. Excuse me, Bob? Sorry to interrupt, but can I just ask —
BOB. Please wait.
TED. No, this is just a little thing. But. Shouldn't the finisher be last? *(Bob stares at Ted.)* Because finisher means it's finished. Technically speaking. *(Bob keeps staring at Ted.)*
BOB. I don't understand.
JAMIE. *(To Ted, annoyed.)* It's because I'm the wrapper. I'm going to be wrapping the sandwich.
BOB. *(Panicking.)* No no no, we are not there yet.
TED. Yeah, but then you should be called the finisher —
JAMIE. No, because it's not finished until the wrapper wraps it —
TED. Right, but finisher should be the last —
JAMIE. Right but once it's wrapped —
BOB. We are not getting into that yet —
TED. Exactly, that's what I'm saying —
BOB. Stop everyone!
JAMIE. But after you wrap it, you can't do anything else to it. After the sandwich is wrapped you can't finish it.
TED. Why not?
BOB. Stop going ahead!
JAMIE. Because it's wrapped —
TED. But then why am I called —
JAMIE. Because it's fucking wrapped in motherfucking paper. *(A pause. Bob looks very, very upset. Verge of tears.)*
BOB. Please, everyone. Please be friends.
TED. I just thought Bob could be reading the instructions wrong. *(To Bob.)* Go ahead, sir. Please continue. The finisher. Who comes second. *(Bob stares down into the book. Composes himself.)*

BOB. The finisher. The finisher will add the essential product. Meats, including: Turkey, Ham, Honey-Baked Ham, Spicy Ham, Pepperoni, Salami, Pepperoni-Salami Blend, Pulled Pork, Smoky Chicken, Spicy Chicken, Chicken. Bleu Cheese, Pepper Jack Cheese, Cheddar Cheese, Extra Cheese, Caesar Cheese Blend … Etcetera. He will also add the seasonings, of which there are twenty-five varieties, including … Guacamole … Etcetera. If requested, make it a combo. Sub portions for pre-weighs and tuna, see chart. Onions must be no longer than two inches and one-eighth inch thick. Tomatoes must be no more than one-sixth inch thick. Lettuce must not exceed four ounces per sandwich. Meats must not exceed three ounces per sandwich. Tuna mix must not exceed three ounces per sandwich. Bacon must never be broken or cut in half.

TED. Got it.

BOB. Finally, the wrapper shall wrap the sandwich. *(A pause.)* Every sandwich must be completed in under twenty seconds or less.

TED. Excuse me, Bob?

BOB. What?

TED. No, sorry, it's just … That's impossible.

BOB. Why?

TED. What about the toasted ones?

BOB. Every sandwich must be completed in under twenty seconds or less.

TED. But, but Bob, how is that possible if a toaster takes —

BOB. *(Barks.)* Every sandwich must be completed in under twenty seconds or less!

TED. Right, but —

BOB. EVERY SANDWICH MUST BE COMPLETED IN UNDER TWENTY SECONDS OR LESS. *(A pause.)*

TED. *(Under his breath.)* Impossible.

JAMIE. You say impossible. I say inspiring. *(A pause. Bob glares, then goes back to the book.)*

BOB. Operational Procedures, Brand Identity, and Standards, to be followed at all times, no exceptions: Team members must bathe regularly. Team members may not work if they have contagious illnesses. Open sores and wounds must be completely covered. *(He looks up. They all look at each other.)* Team members must always pick up the telephone after the first ring. Team members must NEVER EAT THE INVENTORY. Crisis Situations: Level Three guest complaints, food-borne illness, allergies, infectious disease,

disease, theft, vandalism, robbery, natural disaster, hurricane, tornado, flood, earthquake, fire, power outage, bomb threat, drive-by shooting, and/or customer choking, please follow procedures and checklists on pages one-thirty-seven through one-forty-four. *(They all look unsettled.)* It's all right, everyone. Do not worry. In my country, I was doctor. Dermatologist. *(Bob takes a breath. Turns a page in the manual. Moving on.)*

Scene 3

Ted, Sheri, and Jamie stand in a line behind the counter. Bob is nearby, holding a stopwatch.

BOB. And … *(Bob blows a whistle. They start to make a sandwich for an imaginary customer: Sheri takes a roll of bread, squirts condiments on it, and passes it to Ted. Ted puts meat, cheese, lettuce, etcetera on the bread. Ted passes the sandwich to Jamie, who wraps it.)*

JAMIE. Done.

BOB. Twenty-two seconds. Again! *(They start over. Sheri takes the bread. Ted does the condiments, more focused now, but he can't separate the cheese slices. He panics. Jamie wraps it.)*

JAMIE. Done.

BOB. Twenty-five seconds! *(They are all devastated. At last, they rally, and the process begins again, with even more focus.)*

JAMIE. Done!

BOB. Nineteen seconds!!! *(They all high-five. Bob applauds heartily. Ted pulls Jamie in for a hug. He hugs her a little too long. Sheri sighs.)*

Scene 4

The store is now ready to open. New signs display large photos of tasty sandwiches. They say things like: "How 'Bout a Prime Rib!" and "AvocaDOHHHHH!" and "BACON!" Artificial plants hang from the walls. The Coke machine is illuminated. A large banner reads: "Grand Opening!"

Sheri enters, shivering, in dirty pajamas. Ted is already there, wearing his store uniform, poring over a manual.

TED. Harvest Chicken. Go.
SHERI. Um … Chicken?
TED. *(Closes his eyes.)* Honey-Dijon Chicken, grapes, apples, dried cranberries, cucumbers, pumpkin seeds, spring mix lettuce, and Açai Vinaigrette. Served on mulitgrain flatbread, white, wheat, Rosemary Parmesan, or Chipotle Jack.
SHERI. Chipotle Jack?
TED. Yes.
SHERI. That's a bread?
TED. Yes.
SHERI. *(Extremely disturbed.)* It sounds like a cheese. *(Sheri goes behind a door to change into her uniform.)*
TED. Sheri? It is Sheri, right?
SHERI. Yeah.
TED. I don't mean to pry but … Is everything all right?
SHERI. Everything? I don't know. I doubt it.
TED. No, it's just, you seem a little run-down, if you don't mind my saying so. *(She comes back out, wearing her uniform.)*
SHERI. It's just 'cause I work nights. At the El Taco.
TED. Oh. Where's that?
SHERI. Other side of the mall.
TED. Never been.
SHERI. It's just tacos.
TED. How late do you go over there?
SHERI. Four.

TED. Four in the morning?
SHERI. Yeah.
TED. And you're back here at seven?
SHERI. Yeah.
TED. When do you sleep?
SHERI. Depends if I drive home. Mostly I'll just crash in my car in the parking lot.
TED. That's got to be rough.
SHERI. It's a full-leather interior.
TED. I meant the hours.
SHERI. It's not exactly by choice, you know?
TED. What do you mean?
SHERI. Just that one job's not enough.
TED. To what …
SHERI. I have my dad. He has, like, medications and stuff.
TED. What's wrong with him? Not that it's any of my business —
SHERI. You're right, it's not your business.
TED. You can just tell me if I'm prying —
SHERI. You're prying.
TED. Seriously, just shut me up —
SHERI. Shut up.
TED. Okay.
SHERI. *(Feels bad.)* Listen, um … Sir? The thing is. I'm not really here to make friends.
TED. I'm sure you have enough friends.
SHERI. No.
TED. Oh.
SHERI. But I just want to like, do my job here and not get fired with the least amount of energy possible so I can have energy left over for the taco place, which is where my real passion lies.
TED. But what about school or —
SHERI. I'm eighteen. And anyway, I'm not, you know …
TED. What?
SHERI. Smart. *(Jamie enters with her headphones on, in a tiny mini-skirt and stilettos. She is singing the chorus of something she only half knows the words to. Ted watches her walk through the store. She looks incredibly hot.)*
TED. Tell you a secret?
SHERI. No thanks.
TED. That's the kind of thing I used to really fall for. Back in the day.

SHERI. Huh.
TED. Yep, that is the kind of thing that would have driven me crazy with … *(Makes a gesture/noise.)*
SHERI. Yeah. *(Ted checks his watch and turns the sign on the door to "OPEN.")*
TED. Luckily, I'm happily married now. Two kids.
SHERI. Uh-huh.
TED. Yep. It's great. I do not look around anymore. *(Jamie comes back in, wearing her uniform. Ted is deep in a fantasy.)*
JAMIE. What?
TED. Nothing.
JAMIE. Good. Happy Grand Opening, bitches. Let's make some motherfucking sandwiches. *(They put on their plastic gloves and line up behind the counter. Muzak plays. Outside, the sun moves through the sky until it is night. Ted turns the sign on the door to "CLOSED.")*

Scene 5

Night. Jamie mops. Ted wipes down tables. During the following, Sheri enters and exits with the grease trap vacuum, food containers, and various cleaning implements.

TED. *(Re: her mopping.)* Whoops, missed a spot. I think you missed a spot.
JAMIE. Yep.
TED. You might want to go back and get that.
JAMIE. Nope.
TED. Just that little eency spot over there, see under the —
JAMIE. Yep.
TED. Might just want to go take care of —
JAMIE. Nope.
TED. Don't do it now, just keep doing what you're doing there. I'll keep an eye on it for you. I got your back.
JAMIE. Great.
TED. Well, it's just teamwork. Workin' as a team, and I for one feel

pretty darn proud of this little group we've got here. First day. Strong showing, people. I think we had some pretty happy customers — like that nice-looking elderly lady who came in today, you know, with the scarf, couldn't read the menu, didn't know what to order. So, I suggested an item, she took it to go, and I got the very strong sense that she went home satisfied.

JAMIE. You suggested the Prime Rib.

TED. People like that.

JAMIE. An old lady can't eat Prime Rib. It's a huge sandwich. She probably went home and choked on it.

TED. Okay, thank you for the feedback. Jamie? It is Jamie, right?

JAMIE. Yeah.

TED. Why don't you tell us something you did today that you're proud of?

JAMIE. Well … No.

TED. Why not?

JAMIE. Because I'm not five and this isn't kindergarten.

TED. This is called "recognizing accomplishments." It is proven to be an important morale-boosting trick from the corporate world. I happen to know because it's a world that I spent just a little bit of time in, like say, twenty years.

JAMIE. You did?

TED. I happen to have worked at a little place called ye olde Bank of America? Maybe you've heard of it. And I happen to be in possession of a pesky little thing called an MBA.

JAMIE. No. Really?

TED. Yep.

JAMIE. Wow.

TED. Yes.

JAMIE. That's so sad.

TED. You think? I don't really see it that way.

JAMIE. You have an MBA and you're making sandwiches.

TED. This is temporary, I'm in transition.

JAMIE. Yeah, but you have an actual degree in business and —

TED. It's not some big deal. So I got laid off. Downsized. I look at the positive, this is an opportunity for a fresh start. I work hard here, keep my head down, stay focused, I can learn the business from the bottom up. Before you know it, I can move right up the ladder, maybe wind up in corporate.

JAMIE. Uh-huh. Whatever gets you through the day.

TED. You know what gets me through the day? I think of this guy. Just a regular guy. He's walking on the beach. And after a little while, he looks back at where he's been. He was walking alone. But there's two sets of footprints. His and God's.
JAMIE. Ohhh.
TED. Yeah. But then this guy notices something else. During the tough times in his life, there's only one set.
JAMIE. WHAT?!
TED. And he thinks, "God abandoned me just when times got hard."
JAMIE. Dick.
TED. But, hold on. Then God says, "No, I was carrying you." Boom.
JAMIE. Wow.
TED. Yeah.
JAMIE. And so, like, you're saying God is carrying you right now.
TED. You too, if you need it.
JAMIE. Hey God, I'm — *(Calling.)* I'm all good!
TED. Right.
JAMIE. No, seriously, this is kind of like a dream come true. Ever since I was a little girl I just loved sliced meats.
TED. Right, well, good for you.
JAMIE. Plus like a month ago, I got fucking fired from Supercuts. You know the one in the Fairview Mall?
TED. Sure, yeah, I've been there.
JAMIE. Did they give you that haircut?
TED. Oh. Actually, yeah, I think so.
JAMIE. Fucking Darlene. *(Jamie shakes her head. Ted touches his hair self-consciously.)* Anyway, they said I was stealing mousse. Allegedly.
TED. The hair product?
JAMIE. The animal. So yeah, they were pissed, but for like six weeks, my hair had incredible volume and lift. *(She fluffs her hair.)*
TED. Your hair looks fine now.
JAMIE. Thanks. You really know how to flatter a girl.
TED. What? Good. It looks good.
JAMIE. Nah, I barely even did it today.
TED. It does. It looks good —
JAMIE. *(Flirty.)* No.
TED. Yeah.
JAMIE. Come on —
TED. What? I'm just saying —
JAMIE. What?

SHERI. Um … You guys? *(Jamie and Ted both look at her, having totally forgotten about her existence.)* Sorry, but I have to, um … Sorry.
JAMIE. What?
TED. Everything okay, Sheri?
SHERI. Oh. No, it's just, I did the Toasty Trays and the inventory and the dry storage and the frozen storage and the refrigerated storage? But the door, the door in back? It has an alarm system on it? It's just, what it says to do in the routines log on the operations schedule —
TED. What is it, Sheri?
SHERI. Oh. Um. I don't know the code. To turn on the alarm. Which is what we're supposed to do. That's all.
TED. You're saying we need Bob to give us the code.
JAMIE. Bob? Who's Bob?
TED. Bob. The Boss guy.
SHERI. Right. And he's not here. So …
TED. She has a point.
SHERI. I don't think I have a point —
JAMIE. What's the point?
TED. The guy misses his own Grand Opening? It's pretty strange.
SHERI. That's not really what I was —
JAMIE. *(Ignoring Sheri.)* So he misses one day, so what?
TED. Not just any day. The Grand Opening.
JAMIE. Maybe he didn't feel like it today. I mean, did you feel like coming here today?
SHERI. Um, you guys? I have to get to El Taco —
TED. What if something happened to him?
JAMIE. Like what?
TED. He could have some kind of a problem, a medical problem. He could be lost. He's clearly new to this country —
JAMIE. Oh, come on.
TED. He could have slipped in the shower. He could have banged his head, or had some kind of unusual allergic reaction or —
SHERI. *(Quietly creepy.)* He could be lying somewhere in a pool of his own blood. *(A pause. They both look at Sheri.)*
JAMIE. Or he could be having, like, the best sex of his entire life with a gorgeous stacked supermodel —
SHERI. Anyway, I really have to go.
TED. We should try to check on him. Do we have his phone number? He could need our help —
SHERI. I really just need the code to the —

JAMIE. How are we going to help him?
TED. Well, the first step is to do the responsible thing. I mean, she's right. He could be lying in a pool of his own blood.
JAMIE. Well, if that's the case, he's probably not going to pick up the fucking phone.
SHERI. *(Quietly.)* I was just spitballing.
TED. I'm getting my packet. *(Ted goes into the back.)*
JAMIE. That is seriously the saddest guy I have ever met.
SHERI. I guess.
JAMIE. Do you think I should have sex with him?
SHERI. Why would you —
JAMIE. You know, the Everest thing?
SHERI. What?
JAMIE. Because it's there.
SHERI. Um. I think he's married.
JAMIE. I don't really have a judgment about that.
SHERI. Right, no, it's just, he might.
JAMIE. Doubtful. *(Sheri doesn't move. Ted returns, holding the packet. Jamie reaches for the chips.)*
SHERI. *(To Jamie.)* We're not supposed to eat the inventory.
TED. *(Rifling through the packet.)* Here it is. Emergency contact. *(Looks up.)* Would you call this an emergency? We should call. Who wants to call? I'll call. *(He takes out his cell phone. Dials. A pause. The phone on the wall rings.)* Could somebody get that? You have to pick up after one ring. *(Jamie runs and grabs it.)*
JAMIE. Hello, thank you for calling the home of the Tasty Torpedo. I'm sorry we're … *(Realizing.)* Closed.
TED. *(Into phone.)* Hi.
JAMIE. *(Sexy, breathy.)* Hi.
TED. I'm going to hang up now.
JAMIE. *(Sexy.)* Oh, don't do that, that would be —
TED. Okay. Talk to you later. Bye. *(Ted hangs up. Jamie hangs up. A pause.)* That's the only phone number he put.
JAMIE. So?
TED. We've got no other contact information, no way of tracking him down —
JAMIE. Maybe we should dust for prints.
SHERI. Okay. I have to get to work. Late. Sorry. Um. Bye. *(She grabs her sombrero and awkwardly goes. Ted and Jamie look at each other, suddenly alone together.)*

TED. I guess I should stick around here a bit longer, in case he shows up.
JAMIE. Okay.
TED. Okay what?
JAMIE. Me too.
TED. Oh, no you really don't have to. You must have somewhere to be.
JAMIE. I do. But I don't want to be there.
TED. Oh.
JAMIE. And anyway, sticking around is the right thing to do. As part of the team.
TED. Right.
JAMIE. What?
TED. No, I guess I didn't peg you as such a — committed team member.
JAMIE. I take offense at that. I am a very committed team member.
TED. You are?
JAMIE. Yeah. I'm, like, super-duper committed to the team.
TED. That's great.
JAMIE. It's funny. Sometimes I feel like … I would do anything for the team.
TED. *(Laughs a little.)* Right, sure.
JAMIE. I mean, literally. Anything.
TED. Well … That's nice of you.
JAMIE. Ask me what I'd do. Ask me.
TED. No thanks.
JAMIE. Ask.
TED. That's all right —
JAMIE. Ask.
TED. What would you do?
JAMIE. I would — I mean, you and I could — make fucking hot … Sandwiches. *(She smiles. He gets very uncomfortable.)* Wait. What did you think I was going to say? Don't you have a wife?
TED. And kids.
JAMIE. And kids?
TED. Samantha and Cooper.
JAMIE. Cooper? Is that a kid or a golden retriever?
TED. My wife picked it.
JAMIE. My kids are Dax, Frodo, and Bam Bam.
TED. Really?

JAMIE. No. *(Laughs.)* Loosen up.
TED. What? I'm —
JAMIE. What.
TED. I'm a happily married man.
JAMIE. So?
TED. So I shouldn't —
JAMIE. You shouldn't be alone with a coworker? Can't control yourself?
TED. Of course I can control —
JAMIE. Good. I'm gonna go change out of this uniform.
TED. No, please don't — *(She's gone.)* Fuck. Fuck fuck fuck. Ted. Fuck. Ted Ted Ted. Okay. *(She comes back. She looks incredibly hot.)* So, I try not to put myself in situations where I — // because — I — I should probably, I should, um, I should …
JAMIE. Believe me, I get it.
TED. Oh, thank God.
JAMIE. I do the same thing. I try not to put myself in situations where anything interesting could happen.
TED. That's not what I —
JAMIE. But here's the thing, Phil —
TED. Ted —
JAMIE. Here's the thing. The truth is, when I look back on my life? It's not a beach with footprints, you know what I'm saying?
TED. No.
JAMIE. It's not some salt air and sand and fun in the sun.
TED. Okay …
JAMIE. It's more like, an endless parade of shit?
TED. Excuse me?
JAMIE. A shit parade?
TED. *(As if it's clear now.)* Oh. Sure. Right.
JAMIE. You know what I'm talking about. And we all know what we should do. Just keep walking in that shit parade, holding our shit pompoms or our shit banner, maybe if you're lucky you ride the float — but it's still a shit float, see what I'm saying? A float of shit. Until ultimately you realize that you yourself have become a hard little lump of shit, and all you can hope for at that point is that you avoid disaster, like you don't get cancer. Because the only thing worse than being shit, is being shit with cancer. *(He stares at her.)*
TED. I love my family.
JAMIE. So why are we here?

TED. I can't speak for you, but I'm here in case Bob comes back —
JAMIE. No, why are we really here? *(He thinks.)*
TED. Do you mean here, like, on this planet? Or here, like, in this sub shop?
JAMIE. Both.
TED. I guess to try to … Be happy. Isn't that why we're all here? *(A pause.)*
JAMIE. Do you mean here, like, on this planet? Or here in this sub shop? *(He considers this question very carefully, his eyes locked on her.)*
TED. I guess … Both. *(They look at each other for a long, charged moment. Finally, they start to furiously make out. As they kiss, they awkwardly make their way to the floor. They go at it.)*

Scene 6

During store hours. Muzak plays. Ted, Jamie, and Sheri stand behind the counter. Ted is chopping tomatoes, making sure they are the perfect width. The dull, hammering sound of the knife on the counter, in time to the Muzak. Faster. Slower. Faster.

Jamie and Ted are not looking at each other. Sheri notices the tension. Jamie gives Sheri a look, like: "What?" Sheri shrugs and looks away sheepishly.

Bob bursts in, looking very upset. They all look up.

BOB. Yes. Hello. *(He rushes into the back room. The door slams. The muffled, indecipherable sound of Bob yelling in a foreign language.)*
JAMIE. *(Whispered.)* What the —
TED. *(Whispered.)* Shhhh. He's on the phone. *(Bob comes back in. Sweating. He attempts a smile.)*
BOB. Hello. Everything okay? Everyone is good today? How is the sandwich making? Excellent. See you tomorrow. *(He rushes out. They all look at each other.)*
JAMIE. *(Calling after him.)* Dude. What the fuck? WHAT THE

FUCK? This is your fuckin' franchise! Show up, dude! SHOW UP. *(Pause. Ted makes a decision.)*

TED. I think I should hop on the phone with the Feds.

JAMIE. Hop on the phone with the Feds?

SHERI. Oh, I don't think we need Feds.

TED. We need help. This is bigger than us. I mean, do you have any idea what he was yelling about in there?

JAMIE. No. Do you?

TED. No. That's the whole point.

SHERI. *(Quietly, re: Ted.)* I think you're being kind of, um, racist?

TED. Don't even. I have nothing against the people of — Bob's people. *(Re: Sheri.)* She could be working with him. Maybe that's the real reason she's tired all the time.

SHERI. That's just tacos.

JAMIE. How do you know I'm not working with him?

TED. Are you?

JAMIE. No.

TED. Good. That's what I thought.

JAMIE. But that's exactly what I would say, isn't it Ted? Think about it.

SHERI. If we're going to do anything, we should call corporate.

TED. Call corporate?!?

JAMIE. Now see, that's a reasonable idea.

SHERI. *(Really touched.)* Thanks.

TED. Corporate doesn't have a protocol for this.

SHERI. Okay, but I think we, um, just say we're concerned about Bob, and we're wondering what we should do.

TED. Call corporate. That's just great. All that is necessary for evil to triumph is for normal people to stand by and call corporate.

JAMIE. It's the only thing to do that doesn't make us seem like paranoid lunatics but still makes us seem like we care.

TED. *(Exploding.)* I don't need to seem like I care. I do care. There's a difference.

JAMIE. Great.

TED. Learn about it.

JAMIE. Fine.

TED. Great.

JAMIE. Fine.

TED. Good.

JAMIE. Okay. *(A stand-off.)*

SHERI. Um … The number for corporate is in the packet. I'll go get my packet. *(Sheri goes behind the counter to find her packet.)*
TED. *(Grumbling.)* That's right. Wait for corporate to save us. They'll run this up the flagpole, PowerPoint it, get HR involved, leave word, trade calls, and NOTHING WILL HAPPEN — *(Sheri reads from the packet.)*
SHERI. It actually says, "Direct all inquiries to the regional office."
TED. Even better.
SHERI. And then I guess they call corporate headquarters.
TED. Sure. That's just great. *(Sheri picks up the phone. Ted grabs it from her.)* I'll do it. *(He dials. Listens.)* It's busy.
SHERI. I guess we could try back later?
TED. Fine.
JAMIE. Great.
TED. Way to take action, folks. I just hope you can live with yourselves.
JAMIE. It's no harder than the rest of the shit that we're living with. I mean, case in point.
TED. What case in point?
JAMIE. I don't know, I mean, throw a rock.
TED. To have a case in point, you have to actually point to a case. // That's what "case in point" means —
JAMIE. I don't have to do anything but pay taxes and die, and the taxes part is flexible —
SHERI. *(Suddenly concerned.)* Hey guys?
TED. Right, so why should I expect you to understand what it's like to do the right thing.
JAMIE. Are you kidding? You think that's what you're doing?
TED. There's no question that's what I'm doing.
SHERI. *(Concern mounting.)* Guys?
JAMIE. You're just trying to feel better about your own sad little life by taking some kind of a stand.
TED. My sad little life?
JAMIE. *(Continuing.)* As if that gives you some kind of purpose or meaning.
TED. My sad little life?
JAMIE. You think it makes you big. You think it makes you a good guy. When the truth is, throwing Bob under the bus doesn't make you stronger, and it doesn't make you a good guy. // It just makes you a bully —

SHERI. *(Concern mounting even more.)* Guys?
TED. I don't need something to make me a good guy. I am a good guy.
SHERI. // *(Becoming agonized.)* Guys?
TED. *(Continuing.)* Not that you'd recognize one if he fell right smack on top of you —
JAMIE. You basically did fall right smack on top of me —
TED. You came on to me!
JAMIE. And you think that lets you off the hook?
SHERI. *(More agony.)* Guys?
TED. I go home every night.
JAMIE. Oh, that's great. You go home and lie to your family. That's even better —
SHERI. *(Total agony.)* Guys?
TED. What do you expect from me? Because you don't exactly seem like relationship // material. I mean, I'm sorry if I don't want to settle down with a stealing, manipulative —
JAMIE. Well, you're a bad person, you're not a good —
SHERI. *(At the top of her lungs.)* GUYS! *(A pause. They finally notice her. Ominously.)* I think we're running low on tuna. *(Ted and Jamie look to Sheri. A strange chill goes through the room.)*

Scene 7

The store is closed for the night. Darkness, save for the glow of moonlight and the Coke machine. Sheri, alone, is on the phone. She is on hold. She sits, cradling the receiver in her neck, for a very long time.

SHERI. … Hello? Oh, hi, yes, I was just, I've been on hold? Is this the regional office? Oh, um, Sheri Luntz? From the Oak Park branch? In the Oak Park mall? No, that one is, like, down the road from us? Yeah, there's two, it's just three minutes away? I guess, you know, if one is good, can two be bad? Yeah, it can. No, I know that. Oh, no, I'm just the baser? The baser? The baser? It's, the, I introduce the sandwich to the … Yeah, there's the baser, finisher, wrapper, it's — It's in the packet, if you read the — Never mind. *(A pause.)* Anyway, I, well, at our, um, store, see, one of my co-workers — Right, sandwich artists — Well, actually, let me, the point is, our manager, he hasn't been here in, like, a week and a half, and because it was my idea to call corporate — I mean, right, the regional office — I took off a night of work — Oh, well, who are you? The assistant to the Associate Regional Franchise Consultant? Oh. *(Listens.)* Got it, I see, I get it. That's a lot of responsibility. So, do you have any idea what we should — Just stay open? Okay. Just. Stay. Open. And you'll take a message. And on the message, could you also say that, I think we were supposed to get, like a delivery of some sandwich meats? And it didn't show up. And it's just, without the, like, tuna and turkey and stuff — Me? Oh, I always liked the Southwestern Chicken. Yeah, most people say the Prime Rib. Okay. Take care, you too. Okay. Thank you. Thanks so much. Bye. *(She slowly hangs up.)*

Scene 8

Sheri, Ted, and Jamie behind the counter. Muzak plays. A customer in a baseball cap is reading the menu.

CUSTOMER. … Lemme get the, ah, Prime Rib value combo, with barbecue potato chips, an oatmeal cookie, and a Diet Coke. *(Sheri, Ted, and Jamie all look down with a mix of dread and despair. At last, Sheri looks up.)*
SHERI. Um … White or wheat?
CUSTOMER. Doesn't it come on sourdough?
SHERI. The Prime Rib?
CUSTOMER. Yeah. It says up there it comes on toasted sourdough.
SHERI. Yeah, it's just, um, the thing is —
JAMIE. We're all out of sourdough.
CUSTOMER. Okay. I'll have it on … Chipotle Jack.
SHERI. We're, um …
JAMIE. We only have white and wheat.
SHERI. We actually only have wheat.

JAMIE. We were supposed to get a bread delivery but —

TED. We're in a situation here. It may be global, it may be specific, it may be small potatoes, it may be a big deal. We've been in contact with the regional office —

CUSTOMER. Fine, whatever, you know what? Make it a turkey on wheat.

JAMIE. We don't have turkey.

CUSTOMER. You don't have turkey? How is that possible?

TED. I hear you, sir. We might still have ham?

JAMIE. We're out of ham.

CUSTOMER. You're out of ham. You're out of turkey and ham and sourdough —

JAMIE. And swiss and Jack and cheddar.

SHERI. No, we have cheddar. I think — *(Checking.)*

CUSTOMER. I don't want cheddar. Why would I want cheddar?

TED. You don't have to have cheddar.

SHERI. *(Finding it.)* We do have cheddar.

CUSTOMER. Great. Congratulations. But I want a Prime Rib value combo on a sourdough roll with barbecue chips and an oatmeal cookie and a Diet Coke!

TED. I understand, sir.

SHERI. It's just, Prime Rib's our most popular —

JAMIE. Was.

SHERI. Was our most popular —

JAMIE. We don't have it anymore. We're out of it. Finished. Done. Get over it.

CUSTOMER. Is this some kind of a joke?

JAMIE. No.

CUSTOMER. Am I on Candid Camera? Is, like, Ashton Kutcher punking me or something —

JAMIE. Ashton Kutcher punks celebrities. Are you a celebrity? 'Cause if you were, I don't think you'd be here, ordering a value combo —

TED. Jamie, please.

JAMIE. What? The guy should know if he matters enough to be fucked with by a celebrity on TV.

CUSTOMER. Do you matter enough to get fucked with by a celebrity on TV?

JAMIE. No, when I get fucked there's about zero entertainment value —

TED. Sir. I understand your frustration.

CUSTOMER. *(To Ted.)* Are you the manager?
TED. No.
CUSTOMER. Let me talk to the manager.
JAMIE. There's no manager —
TED. There is a manager, he's just not here —
SHERI. He disappeared.
CUSTOMER. He disappeared. How did he disappear?
TED. If we knew the answer to that —
CUSTOMER. People don't just disappear. There are laws of physics that state that.
JAMIE. // Oh, so now you're a physicist?
TED. There's another franchise under three minutes away if you —
CUSTOMER. I don't want to drive three minutes away. Do you not respect my time?
JAMIE. Have a cheese on wheat.
CUSTOMER. Does that sound delicious to you? 'Cause it sounds to me like I'm back in the fucking fifth-grade cafeteria.
TED. Sir, that's not necessary —
CUSTOMER. You people have a lot of nerve, you know that? To be standing here, with the store open —
SHERI. Because the regional office told us // to stay open —
CUSTOMER. Do you always do everything everyone tells you? Are you six fucking years old? WAKE UP! MAKE IT A COMBO!
TED. Sir, we can't —
CUSTOMER. *(Even more enraged.)* You suck. YOU PEOPLE ARE FUCKED UP AND YOU SUCK!!!!!!!!!! Fresh and toasty. My. Ass. *(And he's gone. Everybody just stares. Jamie looks very upset.)*
JAMIE. FUUUUUUCK YOUUUUUUU! *(She starts to break down.)* I'm just — I'm fine — I'm just tired of getting yelled at. *(She grabs a napkin. Wipes her face. Melting down more.)* That other lady today, when I told her we were out of Dr. Pepper, she threw a napkin dispenser at my head. It's like, what is wrong with people? What is everyone getting so angry for? It's like, it's the middle of the day. It's lunch. It's just fucking lunch.
TED. People just get angry when they aren't getting what they want.
JAMIE. *(Exploding at him.)* I'm not getting what I want either. I'm not getting what I want. I have never ever gotten what I want.
TED. Jamie. I have a wife and kids, I don't know what you want me to —
JAMIE. I'm not talking about you, you nitwit. I'm not upset

because of one late night mistake. It's more the life-long mistake I'm dealing with here. *(Ted and Sheri stare at Jamie, not sure what to do.)*

SHERI. Maybe we should close?

TED. What?

SHERI. The store, I mean. Bob's not coming back. So maybe we should just close —

JAMIE. Close the store?

TED. The regional office said to stay open.

SHERI. That guy was right.

JAMIE. That guy was a dick —

SHERI. We have no sandwich stuff. We're a sandwich store. It makes no sense. We make no sense.

JAMIE. Speak for yourself —

TED. Okay, whoa whoa whoa. People. Let's not, let's just, um assess the situation before we make a drastic move here. Now there's a list of distributors on the wall in Bob's office —

SHERI. I already called the distributors. They said all the payments stopped coming. And when they asked why. They were told the account was way, um, overdrawn?

TED. I'm not sure I follow.

SHERI. Nobody's been making deposits into the account.

TED. Uh-huh.

SHERI. And so now there's no money to pay for the food, and so once we run out of the food that we have left, we'll have nothing.

TED. Well, we have the cash from the register —

SHERI. We can maybe pay off what we owe the distributors, but then, we won't get paid and then, I mean, yeah, once we run out of stuff. We're out of work. No one's coming to save us.

TED. What about the other franchise three minutes away —

JAMIE. They don't care about us. They're the competition — they want us to fail. Don't you get it? We've been abandoned. There's one set of footprints.

TED. Well, there'd be three.

JAMIE. The point is, nobody's carrying us. There's nobody there. Watching out for us.

SHERI. We're all alone.

JAMIE. You're fine. You still have El Taco.

SHERI. That's just tacos.

JAMIE. It's more than just tacos. It's a job. You still have a life.

You understand? Of course you don't understand, you're twelve fucking years old. Look at me, I'm thirty-three, I have three kids, and — and I'm in a custody battle, and if I don't have work, if I'm unemployed, I'll lose my kids. Do you get that? I'll lose my kids.
SHERI. You'll find something else.
JAMIE. Where? What else? I can't even get hired by anyone who, you know, actually checks references. Not to mention, my youngest, for his birthday, he's got his heart set on this bike. It's this green, little kid's dirt bike, it costs seventy-nine ninety-nine.
SHERI. I don't know what to —
JAMIE. What am I supposed to tell my son? Huh? "You can't have a bike"? Seventy-nine ninety-nine. What the fuck?
SHERI. I'm sorry. There's nothing I can do. *(A pause. Sheri takes her sombrero and goes. Jamie and Ted are alone.)*
JAMIE. Don't say anything. Just, anything that you could say right now is only going to make it worse.
TED. Okay.
JAMIE. Well, say something.
TED. What?
JAMIE. I don't know. At least try to cheer me up a little. *(Ted thinks.)*
TED. I think you need to work on your attitude.
JAMIE. Excuse me?
TED. Maybe if you just thought a little more positive —
JAMIE. Really? How's that working for you, Ted? Because you're practically fifty —
TED. Forty-three.
JAMIE. I mean, you have an MBA —
TED. There were layoffs —
JAMIE. And you're stuck making sandwiches. I mean how stupid does a guy have to be —
TED. You're just lashing out —
JAMIE. How fucking retarded —
TED. It was downsizing —
JAMIE. Not everyone got laid off, Ted. There are plenty of people with business degrees who make money, lots of money. And I'm sick of you walking around here with your bullshit advice, your positive attitude, and your fucking briefcase like you're better than this —
TED. I am better than this! FUCK. *(Pause. Seething.)* I was a big fish! In a fairly decent-sized pond!

JAMIE. Oh yeah? Then how the fuck are you here?
TED. I have no idea! I don't know — It's like one day you wake up — and you realize, your choices have stuck. Your kid brother looks old. Your closet is full of Land's End pajamas —
JAMIE. So what?
TED. So I made some mistakes, I — screwed up, screwed around. She was — I was her boss — she went to HR — that was it. I got tagged with it. Word gets around. Next thing I know, my wife packed up our things, the kids, her little jar with my balls in it, and made us all move to the middle of nowhere to live with her parents. The whole place smells like milk and Depends. Half the reason I even come here is just to get out of the house … This fucking place … It's all I have. Anyway. Now you know what a loser I am.
JAMIE. Yeah. *(A beat, then.)* Before this, I had no idea.
TED. Ha. Right.
JAMIE. Right. *(They hold each other's gaze. A moment of connection.)*

Scene 9

Sheri, alone in the store, late, late at night. She is fast asleep, her head on one of the tables, her sombrero next to her. Suddenly, an odd haze fills the room …

There is a knock at the door. Again. Again. Sheri starts to stir, groggy.

SHERI. What? Hello? *(Through the glass pane in the door, just barely visible in the haze, is an enormous, human-sized, toasted sub sandwich. The sandwich knocks again.)* Oh. Sorry. We're closed for the night. *(But the door creaks open and the sandwich walks in.)* I said we're closed, sir. You'll have to come back another — *(The sandwich doesn't move.)* I'm only here because I worked late at El Taco, and it was too cold in my car. I'm probably not supposed to — Sir? Sir. You have to leave.
SANDWICH. Hello there.
SHERI. Are you selling something?
SANDWICH. No.

SHERI. Then why are you dressed like a sandwich?
SANDWICH. I am a sandwich.
SHERI. No, but why are you …
SANDWICH. Because. I am.
SHERI. Oh. Huh. *(Sheri stares at him. She is somewhere between kind of dazed and really freaked out.)* You're a really big sandwich.
SANDWICH. Or you're a really small person.
SHERI. Good point. *(The sandwich looks at the menu.)* We're out of most things, I'm sorry. I think we still have some cheddar.
SANDWICH. What do you think, I'm some kind of cannibal?
SHERI. What? *(Understanding.)* Oh. So, what do you eat then?
SANDWICH. Lots of things. Mostly … fear.
SHERI. Nobody eats fear.
SANDWICH. I do. I'm eating your fear right now.
SHERI. Oh. *(The sandwich takes a deep breath.)* Thanks.
SANDWICH. You're welcome.
SHERI. What does it taste like?
SANDWICH. Chicken.
SHERI. Really?
SANDWICH. It's a bit dry. Can I get a Diet Coke?
SHERI. Um … Sure. *(She goes to the soda machine. Remembering.)* We're actually all out of everything but Vanilla Coke. Everybody hates Vanilla Coke, so we still have it.
SANDWICH. *(Declaiming.)* Thou preparest a table before me in the presence of mine enemies. Thou anointest my head with oil, balsamic vinegar, and twenty-five other seasonings … Etcetera, etcetera. My cup runneth over with Diet Coke. *(Sheri tries the Diet Coke soda fountain. It works.)*
SHERI. Diet Coke. That actually worked. *(She hands the soda to the sandwich.)*
SANDWICH. Straw. *(She hands him a straw.)* Thank you. *(He slurps his Diet Coke.)*
SHERI. Can you also maybe, like, fill up the counter with meats and stuff? Because we need pretty much everything —
SANDWICH. Only you can do that, Sheri.
SHERI. What? You mean —
SANDWICH. Only you can fill up that counter with meats and stuff.
SHERI. Me? No, I don't —
SANDWICH. Find the power within you.
SHERI. How? I'm just the baser.

SANDWICH. The baser is important.
SHERI. Why?
SANDWICH. You introduce the sandwich.
SHERI. I guess. Oh. *(Making an introduction.)* And your name is?
SANDWICH. Prime Rib.
SHERI. That's the most popular kind.
SANDWICH. I know.
SHERI. I'm Sheri. *(They shake hands. Sheri seems to recognize something new in herself, or in the world. She stands up a tiny bit straighter. A disco ball effect begins in the room. Very romantic Muzak begins to play. The sandwich offers his hand. They begin a sweet, slow dance. Sheri puts her head on his shoulder. The tiniest smile creeps over her face. It's magic.)*

Scene 10

Cardboard, handwritten signs are now up all over the store. They say things like: "NO MORE PRIME RIB! SORRY!" "We are out of ALL soda except Vanilla Coke! SORRY!" "We are probably out of what you want! SORRY!" "WE HAVE BEEN ABANDONED BY CORPORATE," and "PLEASE DO NOT BE MAD AT US."

Ted is on the phone. Sheri is sitting near him, writing and doing math on a legal pad.

TED. *(Into the phone.)* No sir. No. I'm just asking for turkey and ham. Right, on credit. Okay, fine, forget turkey, I'll make you a deal, 'cause I'm in a good mood, it's just ham. Just advance me some ham. Sir. Please. Advance me some ham. It's just ham. Just advance me some — Don't make me beg. Okay, fine, sir, I'm begging you — Advance me some ham — No, please, don't hang up — *(Ted slams down the phone.)* Goddamnit, these people.
SHERI. Uh-huh.
TED. These goddamn people.
SHERI. Mmm-hmmm.

TED. The guy won't even advance me some ham.
SHERI. Oh.
TED. He was the last of the pre-approved distributors. Did you know that we are only allowed to use their pre-approved distributors?
SHERI. Yeah, 'cause there's that list // in the —
TED. But do you know what else?
SHERI. They're more ex // pensive.
TED. *(As if Sheri had not spoken.)* They're more expensive. They charge you, the franchisee —
SHERI. Forty // cents extra —
TED. Forty cents extra per pound. And it all goes to a kickback to corporate. No wonder Bob bolted. The poor guy had no chance.
SHERI. Yeah, 'cause they sold // him the franchise —
TED. 'Cause they sold him the franchise, it cost, hello —
SHERI. Over four hundred and fifty —
TED. Over four hundred and fifty thousand dollars! But what he didn't know — IS THAT YOU HAVE NO CONTROL — they can put your store wherever they want — any crappy, impossible, dead-end location, they can wait up to —
SHERI. Two // years —
TED. Two years to open it. They set all the prices, they control the supply chain. It's all on their terms! They basically have you by the balls. They sell you the store; you give them your balls. How is that fair? What the hell kind of world do we live in? Where people just … People just … Take people's … Forget it. I give up. I give up. *(Ted is in despair.)*
SHERI. Yeah. Listen, Ted. *(A deep breath.)* I know things are maybe a little stressful for you these days …
TED. I'm not stressed out. I'm suicidal.
SHERI. Okay, great. But. Um. In spite of that. I'm hoping we can all still work together, because I, I had this really weird dream …
TED. You had a dream?
SHERI. Right. And I think what it meant was, well, I had this idea and I think it could save — *(Jamie comes in, carrying A&P grocery bags. She plunks them on the tables. Starts handing Sheri change.)*
JAMIE. They had turkey on special, so I got a ton of that. And then I got peanut butter, jelly, um, a bunch of bread —
TED. *(To Jamie.)* You went to the supermarket?
JAMIE. *(Re: Sheri.)* She sent me.
SHERI. Yeah, um, that's what I —

TED. You sent her to the supermarket?!?
SHERI. Yeah. 'Cause we're out of food, so?
TED. That was your big idea? Peanut butter and jelly?
SHERI. Well, among other things.
TED. You can't just do that.
JAMIE. Why not?
SHERI. It's just until —
TED. People have expectations. We're a franchise. You can't just sell — *(He rifles through the bag.)* Crest Whitestrips?
JAMIE. What?
SHERI. What the —
JAMIE. I'll pay you back. God.
TED. Look, this would be cute if we were twelve and having a bake-sale, but there's a menu, with choices —
JAMIE. Hey, don't look at me —
TED. We can't just, what, sit around here playing house with week-old turkey from the A&P —
JAMIE. It looks fine. It's not even that gray —
TED. Not to mention, it's probably illegal, with the Food and Drug —
JAMIE. Oh no, here he goes, call the Feds —
TED. Don't even —
JAMIE. What? Even what —
SHERI. Stop! Could both of you just stop?! *(This is the loudest Sheri has ever been. Both Ted and Jamie are stunned.)* Look. I never said it was perfect. And if anybody has a better idea, I am more than happy to hear it. But I was doing the numbers and if we sell enough of these sandwiches, our own sandwiches, made however we want, we can make payroll and we'll all be able to hang in there until we get a new owner who will hopefully have some money to invest in buying supplies again, and then we can all go back to, like, normal. It's this or we're out of a job, so … *(To Ted.)* You're the one who said they have us by the balls. Well, let's take our balls back. Take back our balls. *(They both stare at her.)*
TED. I just think it's ridiculous. It's absurd.
SHERI. So?
TED. So? People will laugh at us.
JAMIE. No offense, Ted, but they were laughing already. Have you taken a look at yourself in that vest?
TED. I can't do it. I wouldn't even know how.

SHERI. You can learn.
TED. No, this is too crazy —
JAMIE. Too crazy? For the guy who threw me down on the floor of this sub shop?
TED. I'm not proud of myself.
JAMIE. Well, get proud of yourself.
SHERI. YEAH!
JAMIE. Make your own goddamn sandwich. *(Ted thinks about this.)*
TED. What if they suck?
JAMIE. They won't suck.
SHERI. I make a really kick-ass tuna salad.
TED. You do?
SHERI. It's my biggest skill. *(Pause.)*
TED. I do like a good tuna salad. *(Jamie takes some cans of tuna out of the shopping bag and puts them on the counter.)*
JAMIE. I also stole some mini Snickers. Just for us. *(They look at her.)*
TED. Well … Pass 'em around.
SHERI. Yeah. Hook me up.
JAMIE. That's right. Satisfaction. *(She rips open the bag of candy and shares it with Ted and Sheri as the Muzak swells. Sheri unloads the groceries.)*

Scene 11

The remnants of the homemade sandwich-making are everywhere: Ziploc bags of chips, jars of peanut butter, etc. New cardboard signs read: "PB & J!" "Carrot sticks!" "Sheri's Tuna Salad," and "HOMEMADE SANDWICHES!!!"

Sheri, Jamie, and Ted are working together. All three of them have customized their uniforms, each in his or her special way.

SHERI. … So that's six tuna, six peanut butter and jelly, six turkey and swiss, six just plain butter. Yeah sure, we could cut off the crusts. No, that's not extra. *(Off Ted, glaring at her.)* Okay, that's like ten cents extra. You want a cookie? Yeah, you're right, I know, I'm trying to do the same, but I just sometimes like something sweet at the end of a meal. Me? *(Giggles.)* You're too kind. The tuna? It just has celery and some relish. Seriously, that's the whole secret. Well, I'm glad you enjoy it. Okay, you take care too. Sure, we're closing up but Ted'll drop it all off on his way home … Thanks. Buh-bye. *(Jamie is singing as she works, something like "What's So Funny 'Bout Peace Love and Understanding."* She finishes her song.)* Hey, guys, we have one last delivery for those frat boys over on Hawthorne? I think they might be stoned.

JAMIE. I'm thinking they might be into Sheri.

SHERI. No way.

JAMIE. They're over there at the frat house like, *(As an oversexed frat boy.)* "Yeah, tell her to put some mustard on it, baby."

SHERI. Come on!

JAMIE. "Tell her extra meat."

TED. *(Joining in awkwardly.)* "Want a bite of my tasty torpedo?"

JAMIE. Eeeew.

SHERI. Would you stop? Nobody likes me — I mean, likes me likes me like the way you mean.

JAMIE. That's bullshit. You're a beautiful girl.

SHERI. Anyway, you guys are missing the whole point … You guys! We've sold enough sandwiches that … It's payday. *(Sheri hands out the cash.)*

JAMIE. What? Yes!

TED. Thanks. *(They count their money carefully. Jamie suddenly starts to cry. She looks up, feeling their eyes on her.)*

JAMIE. I'm fine, I'm fine. It's just … This whole thing, I can't fucking believe it … Anyway, fuck YEAH. Let's get out of here. Sheri, verse two, sing us out.

SHERI. Oh. No no no no no. I suck.

JAMIE. How bad could you be?

SHERI. Really bad?

JAMIE. No, come on. I suck.

SHERI. No, you're really good actually.

JAMIE. Thanks. I used to want to be a rock star.

SHERI. And what do you want to be now?

JAMIE. *(Thinks, then.)* A rock star.

SHERI. Well, I'm really, really not … Seriously, guys, I'm not. *(Ted starts to gently drum his fingers on a table or play a peanut butter jar as a bongo, coaxing Sheri along.)*

* See Special Note on Songs and Recordings on copyright page.

JAMIE. Come on. Just try. Try. *(Sheri starts to sing. It's true that Sheri has a really, really bad voice. She sings excruciatingly slowly. And off-key. But with deep, deep feeling. At last, Jamie and Ted join in the singing. They all sing together.)* Yeah, Sheri! Take a bow! *(As Jamie and Ted celebrate Sheri, the door to the store opens. Gregory enters.)*
TED. Hey there, sir.
GREGORY. Am I in the —
TED. Come on in!
SHERI. We were just closing up, but how can we help you?
GREGORY. Oh. Are you sure —
JAMIE. Sure yeah, you look hungry. He looks hungry, am I right?
SHERI. Yeah.
TED. We can take care of that. What would you like?
GREGORY. Prime Rib?
SHERI. Oooh, I'm so sorry.
JAMIE. We're all out of Prime Rib.
TED. Might I recommend peanut butter and jelly?
SHERI. We have turkey, tuna's been super popular, ham, a couple kinds of cheese, and yes, peanut butter and jelly …
JAMIE. Strawberry or grape.
SHERI. Right. We have meatloaf that Ted brought in from home. Jamie's mom made some killer oatmeal cookies, if you want a bag of those.
JAMIE. I have gum in my purse.
SHERI. I brought some Jell-O puddings too, if you want one of those.
TED. *(Remembering.)* And we have Fluffernutters. That's marshmallow fluff, you know, with peanut butter on white. My kids made those last night for school and I nabbed a few. *(Sheri, Ted, and Jamie laugh. Gregory tries to smile along.)*
GREGORY. Harvest Chicken?
SHERI. No.
GREGORY. Southwestern Chicken?
SHERI. Yeah, no. I like that one too.
JAMIE. Dude, read the signs. *(Reading from a cardboard sign.)* "We have been abandoned by corporate … "
GREGORY. Right. Of course. I should introduce myself. Gregory Sharmin. From corporate. *(A pause. Ted, Jamie, and Sheri all look at each other.)*
TED. Ted Cranston. Formerly Bank of America.

SHERI. We've been calling and calling you guys.
GREGORY. Really? I'm so sorry —
TED. We have a very long list of the people we've spoken with at the regional office —
SHERI. We left like a hundred messages —
GREGORY. Oh, well we don't get regional messages over in corporate.
SHERI. You don't?
TED. Man, I hear that. I spent twenty years in the corporate world, and there is so little communication —
GREGORY. Luckily, we finally heard, through some of our operatives in the field —
JAMIE. What operatives in the field?
GREGORY. That we had a franchise out there that had gone rogue.
TED. Whoa, we didn't go rogue.
SHERI. We've been in constant contact with the regional office. They said stay open —
TED. Our franchise owner, he —
SHERI. People come in here hungry, we can't turn them away.
GREGORY. Relax everyone. It's fine. We know what happened.
SHERI. Do you know what happened to Bob?
GREGORY. We don't know what happened to Bob. We know what happened to the franchise.
JAMIE. I bet it's those bitches three minutes away, they ratted us out —
TED. Sorry Greg, sir, I don't think you possibly could — unless you were here, unless you were part of this team —
SHERI. Yeah. Part of the team!
JAMIE. Those fucking bitches, I swear to God, I knew it —
TED. So your source, whoever that was couldn't possibly understand what we — *(Gregory pulls a piece of paper out of his pocket.)*
GREGORY. *(Reads.)* "Dear Corporate, I am writing to alert you to the unfortunate fact that a young woman named Sheri — "
SHERI. With an "i."
GREGORY. A baser. Has concocted a scheme, etcetera —
SHERI. It wasn't a scheme —
GREGORY. *(Still reading.)* "I would like to make clear that the other employees do not approve of this scheme — "
TED. See? This is totally wrong —
GREGORY. "I will send you more insider information — including photos, franchise location, etcetera — for the small price of seventy-

nine ninety-nine, etcetera. Sincerely … Jameson A. McIntyre." *(A stunned pause.)*

SHERI. Jamie?

TED. You sold us out.

JAMIE. No, of course not, I didn't —

TED. Jameson?

JAMIE. I didn't mean —

SHERI. You offered to spy on us?

JAMIE. It's not like that, I —

GREGORY. *(To Jamie.)* Jameson, I presume.

JAMIE. Yeah.

GREGORY. Thank you for alerting us to this unusual and concerning situation.

SHERI. I was trying to alert you the // entire time —

TED. Sheri didn't do anything wrong.

GREGORY. We in corporate are horrified // that something like this could go unnoticed —

TED. We were all in this together.

SHERI. They told us, stay open!

GREGORY. Yes, but this situation flies in the face of everything our brand stands for. // Quality, consistency of product —

JAMIE. No, I didn't, wait — // wait — wait — wait, just WAIT —

TED. I will personally vouch —

SHERI. I spoke with the assistant to the Associate Regional Franchise Consultant!

GREGORY. People, listen to me, what I'm trying to say is, this situation must be addressed —

JAMIE. Wait, please, just please // will you please just stop —

TED. Sir, sir? Back up there sir, // you just back up.

SHERI. At the regional office!

TED. I will personally vouch // for every single thing that we did here, Greg, sir, this is nobody's —

GREGORY. Just hold on everyone! Will you people just listen? I'm simply trying to say it must be addressed —

SHERI. *(Begins after Ted's line, "vouch.")* The regional office! The regional office! The regional office said to stay open!

JAMIE. WAIT — Would all of you please, just STOP!!!!! STOP!!!!! *(Desperate, Jamie wildly seizes a knife from the counter and waves it in no particular direction.)*

SHERI. Jamie. No.

JAMIE. No. It's just. I have something to say. I have something to say. *(Everyone is very quiet.)* Yeah, okay, fuck, I wrote that letter. I don't know. Part of me didn't think they even got mail in corporate.
GREGORY. We get mail. We don't get messages. We get mail.
JAMIE. Well, what the fuck? What is that? Look, I needed to cover my ass, okay? In case we got busted. Us selling people our own homemade sandwiches? I mean, that's insane —
GREGORY. It's illegal.
JAMIE. It's a sandwich.
SHERI. But Jamie, you loved it —
JAMIE. Yeah but this was before, before we even knew it would work. And, you know, sooner or later, I figured we'd all be out of a job. And most likely in trouble. And I, I can't really afford that right now, you know, with my kids and the court case and so I thought that if I could just, you know, seize the opportunity. Because that's what you're supposed to do, right? Stick your neck out, stand out to the guy upstairs.
GREGORY. We know —
JAMIE. No. You don't know. That's my whole point, I mean, have you ever made a Tasty Torpedo? Do you even know what's in the Southwestern Chicken?
GREGORY. I assume chicken.
JAMIE. That's right, you sit there assuming, in your big corporate bubble with your assistant, like, assisting your shit — while we're here, selling "home-baked" cookies and "handcrafted artisan breads" made by fucking machines — all for seven dollars and twenty-five cents an hour. And then there's someone like Sheri —
SHERI. No, I —
JAMIE. A person who actually has a creative idea in her head. And someone like Ted over here —
TED. I'm not —
JAMIE. Who actually cares, who has so much passion inside him that he —
TED. Okay, that's fine —
JAMIE. And together, they figured out how we could still get by. Yeah, survive. These people in front of you, they are the true Sandwich Artists. And I'm not just saying that, you guys, I really mean that. *(They nod thanks.)* And then you think you can just come in here all up on your high horse and try to tear down what we did? Well, I won't let you do that —

GREGORY. That's not what I — *(She impulsively lunges at Gregory.)*
SHERI. Jamie, don't —
TED. Stop, Jamie! *(Gregory dodges, but Jamie's knife catches his jacket, tearing it. Jamie trips and falls hard.)*
GREGORY. What the fuck? *(Jamie, now on the floor, is immediately filled with soul-crushing regret.)*
JAMIE. Shit. Shit shit shit.
GREGORY. You could've killed me —
JAMIE. I'm sorry —
GREGORY. You could've killed me.
SHERI. But she didn't —
GREGORY. She just tried to kill me —
JAMIE. I'm so, so sorry —
GREGORY. Are you insane? You can't just stab someone. That's not okay.
SHERI. No, but she didn't —
GREGORY. You don't go around stabbing people whenever you're pissed off —
SHERI. She's just stressed out —
GREGORY. I don't care. I don't care how stressed out she is. I don't want to get stabbed. *(Checking out the tear in his jacket.)* Goddamnit. This jacket cost a fortune. *(Jamie is standing in a corner now, holding the knife in her shaking hand, crying.)*
JAMIE. I'm sorry.
GREGORY. Stop saying that. Christ.
JAMIE. How can I — I'll make it up to you — Can I —
TED. Jamie. Drop the knife. *(She drops it and sinks to her knees, collapsing on the floor.)*
GREGORY. What is wrong with you?
JAMIE. I know —
GREGORY. I have a family. I coach Little League.
TED. Listen, Greg —
SHERI. She didn't mean it —
GREGORY. What do you people think — do you think I wanted to come here today? Do you think I'm here by choice? Do you think when I was a kid, I was like, hey, maybe one day I'll grow up to be an Associate Manager of Franchise Relations? My dad drove a cab for thirty-five years just to send me to college, first in my family — was this why? So I could end up here? Yay! I'm in corporate! Corporate, where, just FYI, we are three hundred million

in debt — and because of, because of what's going on in this country, not to mention our general ass-backward company policies — none of which I made up or control — just last year we closed six hundred stores. Do you people pay any attention? Read the newspaper! The whole chain was just sold to some creditor to avoid going under. And last month we laid off one hundred and forty people. So yeah, that guy who wasn't returning your calls? It's probably because he was let go. I could be next.

SHERI. *(About to empathize.)* I didn't know —

GREGORY. I'm busting my ass just to keep this job that I hate — dealing with pissed-off franchise owners, all mad at me because of shit I had nothing to do with and can do nothing about — and then, on the weekends my wife is like, "You loaded the dishwasher wrong," and, "I wish you were more affectionate," and "Why can't we afford a bigger TV?" I'm like, "Why aren't you a supermodel? Answer me that." *(Ted and Sheri have no answer for that. They stutter a little.)* But see, I don't say that. That would be mean. And hey, I'm a good guy. I spend what free time I have at the park, with my son's Little League team, trying to teach a bunch of six-year-olds to play baseball. My son sucks. He sucks at baseball. But you know what I do? *(Ted and Sheri shake their heads.)* I take him out after to a Dairy Queen and tell him that I will love him no matter what. And then I go tell my other kids the same thing, so they won't feel weird or left out. And then at night I go to bed, yes, with my wife — who I've been with for seventeen years — who I'm honestly not very attracted to anymore — but I have sex with her anyway — well, sometimes — all because I want her to feel loved too. It's goddamn fatiguing. I'm UNHAPPY. *(Sheri takes a step to comfort him, but he waves her off.)* And that pisses me off. Because I know that I'm lucky. To be here in this country with this set of problems, when my own father grew up in a place where there's not even clean drinking water. We're all lucky to be here, in this particular shit-show — and so, yeah, that's why it sorta pisses me off when, on a day like today, I wake up, kiss my kids, kiss my wife, drive out to wherever the hell we are, and some crazy chick, out of the blue, thinks she has every right to make an attempt on my life —

JAMIE. I didn't —

GREGORY. Because I work in corporate. Because I make more than the minimum wage —

SHERI. That's not what she —

GREGORY. When, in truth, the only reason I'm even here is to tell you that we in corporate would like to reward you, Sheri Luntz — is that right?
SHERI. Yeah.
GREGORY. To reward you, Sheri Luntz, for your bravery, creativity, ingenuity, and service to our company. You are the employee of the month for this whole regional division of the United States! *(A pause.)*
SHERI. I am?
GREGORY. Yes. And we would like to express our gratitude by giving you a prize.
SHERI. Really? Wow, because, I've never won anything before —
GREGORY. Well, today you have. Today, Sheri Luntz, you have won … A trip to our corporate headquarters.
SHERI. Oh. Wow.
GREGORY. Pack your bags, Sheri. You're coming to Denver.
SHERI. I've never been to Denver.
TED. Congrats, Sheri.
SHERI. Thank you. *(Gregory takes out a camera.)*
GREGORY. Get in front of that sign, would you? *(Sheri stands in front of one of her homemade cardboard signs and smiles awkwardly. Gregory snaps a photo. To Ted.)* Get us together? *(He poses next to Sheri. Ted takes a photo of the two of them.)* You leave tomorrow morning. Here's the ticket, all the info. *(Gregory hands Sheri an envelope.)*
TED. We'll man the fort while she's gone.
GREGORY. You'll man the fort. *(Indicating Jamie.)* She is coming with me to see that cop in the parking lot where she will be arrested for some kind of assault with a deadly weapon —
JAMIE. Please, no — my kids, I'm in a — a custody battle. I can't have any more trouble —
GREGORY. Well, maybe you should have thought of that before you assaulted me.
JAMIE. But please, not the cops, not the cops, they'll —
GREGORY. The cops will — deal with this. You're out of control. There are laws, okay? Rules that keep people safe. Without them, it's — I don't know — just — the world wouldn't work. *(To Jamie, who is still on the floor.)* Stand up. I said, stand up. STAND UP. *(Jamie remains crumpled in a heap. Ted walks over to Gregory.)*
TED. *(To Gregory.)* It's okay, Greg. I got this.
GREGORY. Excuse me?

TED. You go get the cop, I can watch over her here 'til you bring the cop in and arrest her. That way we don't have to move her.
JAMIE. What?
SHERI. Ted, that's not —
GREGORY. Hey, look at that. Great idea. Way to think on your feet.
TED. It's just teamwork.
GREGORY. Thank you, my friend. Ted, is it?
TED. Cranston, yes. Ted Cranston.
GREGORY. You know what? Just for that, I am going to snag you an extra ticket to Denver. I want to introduce you around. A guy like you shouldn't be stuck here.
TED. Thank you. I — I can't tell you how much that would mean —
GREGORY. Sure. We could use someone like you. I'll be right back. *(Gregory goes.)*
JAMIE. Ted? What the fuck?
SHERI. How could you?
TED. *(Quietly, to Jamie.)* Go out the back.
JAMIE. What?
TED. The back. Through the alley. Go.
JAMIE. But —
TED. Don't be an idiot. Go. Before he comes back.
JAMIE. But your trip to Denver …
TED. I don't care about Denver.
JAMIE. What? Why not? *(A pause. Ted looks at Jamie with deep feeling.)*
TED. I'll take the heat. I'll figure it out, okay? Just — don't be stupid — don't be an idiot — and try to stop stealing and stabbing people and shit — it's not cool.
JAMIE. Okay.
TED. I … Jamie, I … *(He gently wipes the tears from her face. She looks up at him.)*
SHERI. *(Looking out the front door.)* He's talking to the cop — they're coming back —
JAMIE. Thank you.
SHERI. They're almost here —
TED. *(With love.)* It's okay, Jamie. Go. *(She stares at him, momentarily unable to move.)* Goddamnit. Run. *(At last, Jamie scrambles out the back. Ted watches her go, full of longing. Sheri stands guard. The door swings open, revealing a glimpse of Gregory, entering.)*

Scene 12

Afternoon. Ted makes peanut butter and jelly sandwiches and quietly sings along to the Muzak. He's made a very, very large number of sandwiches. It looks somewhere between industrious and completely obsessive-compulsive.

The front door opens. Sheri enters.

SHERI. Hey.
TED. Hey. How was Denver?
SHERI. It was amazing. Denver's an amazing place.
TED. It sounds amazing. Denver.
SHERI. Yeah.
TED. And you got to meet the CEO?
SHERI. For a minute, yeah.
TED. You guys were on the front page of the Business section.
SHERI. I know! It's so crazy.
TED. They called you an example of what makes America great. "The people. That's 'the special sauce.'"
SHERI. Stupid. *(Pause.)* You hear from Jamie?
TED. Nah. She hated me, anyway.
SHERI. How could she? After what you did, like, stalling them and talking them out of pressing any charges —
TED. It was nothing.
SHERI. It was completely heroic.
TED. *(Shakes his head.)* Well … Thanks. *(The store phone rings. Sheri runs over and picks it up after one ring, as per store rules.)*
SHERI. *(Into phone.)* Hello? *(From the phone, the sound of yelling and screaming in an unidentifiable language.)* Bob? Is that — *(The sound of more yelling and screaming.)* Who? Wait. Slow down. So, wait, who are you then? Sir, I can't understand what you're — No, um, Bob's not here right now.
TED. *(Whispered, to Sheri.)* Take a message.
SHERI. *(Into phone.)* Can I take a message? *(The voice on the phone gets very loud and emphatic. To Ted.)* I don't think they want to

leave a message. *(The voice on the phone goes insane with rage. Then stops.)* Sir? Are you there? *(She hangs up.)*
TED. Yikes. What was that?
SHERI. He just kept yelling about how Bob owes him money, said he was an investor in the franchise.
TED. Well, he'll be back now.
SHERI. You mean —
TED. Bob. He'll come back to recoup his investment. He must have seen the store in the papers. This is a huge marketing opportunity. Do you know how many people came by over the weekend just to check out the store?
SHERI. Really? How many?
TED. Not that many yet, but they will. I mean, why do you think I'm making all these sandwiches? We were all over the internet. We could become a cult sensation.
SHERI. Ted —
TED. I think we have the potential to think creatively and create some real synergy here, like t-shirts saying, "Rogue Subs," or — I have all kinds of ideas —
SHERI. Ted.
TED. What?
SHERI. Well, it's just that … When I flew to corporate … Well, first they gave me a tour of the offices, which basically look like regular offices but with lots and lots of photos of sandwiches. And then they gave me some stuff, like a tote bag and a coupon for ten free Tasty Torpedoes.
TED. Uh-huh.
SHERI. And they showed me where they do focus groups and strategy sessions and think tanks and brainstorms and sandwich testing, where they talk about stuff like sandwich structure and palate satisfaction and optimal mouth-feel.
TED. Okay. Wow.
SHERI. And then finally, I went into the office of the CEO, who was, like, the nicest man in the world. And somebody had done a Starbucks run and gotten me a Grande Frappuccino?
TED. Nice.
SHERI. Which is, like, my favorite drink.
TED. Sure, yeah.
SHERI. And then the CEO asked me a bunch of stuff about myself and we chatted, and it turned out that his mom was a nurse, so that

was cool 'cause that was my plan too, like, once upon a time. And he was like, don't give up on your dream and people like you are what makes America great — And then he started saying how sometimes he really hates his job because there's shareholders and rules and brand management and sometimes you have to do things you don't want to — and it's nobody's fault, it's just how it works — like, in this case, close the store.
TED. What store?
SHERI. Our store.
TED. What? They're closing our —
SHERI. I thought they would have called you —
TED. No.
SHERI. I just came by to pick up my stuff —
TED. But why? Why would they —
SHERI. I guess the regional office can't find a new owner, and it's a terrible location, there's another like three minutes away, so it was never going to be profitable anyway, Bob's smart, I'm sure he figured that out. They only sold it to him 'cause they wanted the franchise fee. They never expected it to succeed. It can't.
TED. Who said that? The CEO guy told you that?
SHERI. He said it was closing. I kind of filled in the rest.
TED. Well, no, they can't just do this —
SHERI. They can do whatever they want —
TED. But, what about us?
SHERI. Don't you have an MBA?
TED. What does that get me? I spent ten months looking for work before I found this situation. I mean, it's easy for you, you have El Taco —
SHERI. I quit El Taco.
TED. What? Why?
SHERI. To travel to Denver. They wouldn't give me the time off.
TED. Are you kidding me? That's insane —
SHERI. Just please don't be mad, okay?
TED. I'm mad at them —
SHERI. Because I already basically feel like a huge piece of crap about everything, so … Please. Don't make it worse. *(A pause.)*
TED. You feel like a huge piece of crap?
SHERI. Yeah basically.
TED. Why?
SHERI. Because.

TED. Okay, but you're smart, you're — one of the smartest people I've ever met in my whole life.
SHERI. Then there's something wrong with your life.
TED. Look, if anyone feels like crap around here, it should be me. At least you got to go to Denver. Look at me.
SHERI. What about you?
TED. Well, for starters, the store's closing, and I just wasted the whole morning making sandwiches. *(Sheri finds this strangely amusing.)* It's not funny.
SHERI. I know, I know.
TED. I just made like a million goddamn sandwiches. *(They both laugh.)* It's absurd. What? It is. What the hell do we do? What do we do with all these stupid goddamn sandwiches? *(A pause. She stops laughing.)*
SHERI. Eat them.
TED. What?
SHERI. You know. Eat the sandwiches. *(Ted considers this.)*
TED. We're not supposed to eat the inventory.
SHERI. I know.
TED. *(A pause. He makes a decision.)* White or wheat?
SHERI. Um —
TED. I got some rye too, actually.
SHERI. You got rye?
TED. My wife bought it by accident and my kids hate rye so … We have peanut butter on white, tuna on rye, Havarti and apple slices on wheat … I know, I went a little off-road. And we have turkey with this cool, like, cranberry mayo? I found the recipe online? You just do a little mustard, some cranberry sauce, some dried cranberries, there's a dash of nutmeg in there — it's fantastic.
SHERI. I'll take one of each.
TED. Coming right up. *(He goes behind the counter and comes back with two paper plates and a gorgeous pile of various sandwiches. He sets the sandwiches on the table in front of Sheri. He grabs Ziploc bags of carrot sticks and chips. And two juice boxes from the fridge. At last, he turns the sign on the door to "CLOSED." He sits down opposite her at the table. They unwrap their sandwiches. These are beautiful, beautiful sandwiches. They are about to take a bite when … The phone rings. Ted leaps up to get it.)*
SHERI. Don't.
TED. But what if it's someone from corporate.

SHERI. So? We're free now. We can do what we want. *(The phone keeps on ringing. He slowly sits back down. She takes a big bite of her sandwich.)* Mmm. This is delicious. *(He takes a bite of his sandwich. Chews, thinking.)*
TED. Freedom.
SHERI. Yeah. Freedom.
TED. Yeah. *(The phone rings again.)*
SHERI. Let it ring. *(She takes a big bite of her sandwich. Finally, the ringing stops. Silence. They eat together, as the lights slowly fade.)*

End of Play

PROPERTY LIST

Large manual
Job application form
Pens and notebooks
Stopwatch
Whistle
Sandwich supplies (bread, condiments, toppings, paper wraps)
Printed display signs
Cardboard handwritten signs
"Grand Opening" banner
Ziploc bags of carrot sticks and chips
Paper plates
Juice boxes
Headphones
Door "Open/Closed" sign
Plastic gloves
Mop
Rag
Vacuum
Food containers
Cell phone
Sombrero
Knife
Napkins
Cups of soda
Straws
Camera
A&P grocery bags
Cash
Mini Snickers
Cans of tuna
Jars of peanut butter
Homemade sandwiches

SOUND EFFECTS

Muzak
Phone ringing
Knock on the door

NEW PLAYS

★ **THE PICTURE OF DORIAN GRAY by Roberto Aguirre-Sacasa, based on the novel by Oscar Wilde.** Preternaturally handsome Dorian Gray has his portrait painted by his college classmate Basil Hallwood. When their mutual friend Henry Wotton offers to include it in a show, Dorian makes a fateful wish—that his portrait should grow old instead of him—and strikes an unspeakable bargain with the devil. [5M, 2W] ISBN: 978-0-8222-2590-4

★ **THE LYONS by Nicky Silver.** As Ben Lyons lies dying, it becomes clear that he and his wife have been at war for many years, and his impending demise has brought no relief. When they're joined by their children all efforts at a sentimental goodbye to the dying patriarch are soon abandoned. "Hilariously frank, clear-sighted, compassionate and forgiving." *–NY Times.* "Mordant, dark and rich." *–Associated Press.* [3M, 3W] ISBN: 978-0-8222-2659-8

★ **STANDING ON CEREMONY by Mo Gaffney, Jordan Harrison, Moisés Kaufman, Neil LaBute, Wendy MacLeod, José Rivera, Paul Rudnick, and Doug Wright, conceived by Brian Shnipper.** Witty, warm and occasionally wacky, these plays are vows to the blessings of equality, the universal challenges of relationships and the often hilarious power of love. "CEREMONY puts a human face on a hot-button issue and delivers laughter and tears rather than propaganda." *–BackStage.* [3M, 3W] ISBN: 978-0-8222-2654-3

★ **ONE ARM by Moisés Kaufman, based on the short story and screenplay by Tennessee Williams.** Ollie joins the Navy and becomes the lightweight boxing champion of the Pacific Fleet. Soon after, he loses his arm in a car accident, and he turns to hustling to survive. "[A] fast, fierce, brutally beautiful stage adaptation." *–NY Magazine.* "A fascinatingly lurid, provocative and fatalistic piece of theater." *–Variety.* [7M, 1W] ISBN: 978-0-8222-2564-5

★ **AN ILIAD by Lisa Peterson and Denis O'Hare.** A modern-day retelling of Homer's classic. Poetry and humor, the ancient tale of the Trojan War and the modern world collide in this captivating theatrical experience. "Shocking, glorious, primal and deeply satisfying." *–Time Out NY.* "Explosive, altogether breathtaking." *–Chicago Sun-Times.* [1M] ISBN: 978-0-8222-2687-1

★ **THE COLUMNIST by David Auburn.** At the height of the Cold War, Joe Alsop is the nation's most influential journalist, beloved, feared and courted by the Washington world. But as the '60s dawn and America undergoes dizzying change, the intense political dramas Joe is embroiled in become deeply personal as well. "Intensely satisfying." *–Bloomberg News.* [5M, 2W] ISBN: 978-0-8222-2699-4

NEW PLAYS

★ **BENGAL TIGER AT THE BAGHDAD ZOO by Rajiv Joseph.** The lives of two American Marines and an Iraqi translator are forever changed by an encounter with a quick-witted tiger who haunts the streets of war-torn Baghdad. "[A] boldly imagined, harrowing and surprisingly funny drama." –*NY Times.* "Tragic yet darkly comic and highly imaginative." –*CurtainUp.* [5M, 2W] ISBN: 978-0-8222-2565-2

★ **THE PITMEN PAINTERS by Lee Hall, inspired by a book by William Feaver.** Based on the triumphant true story, a group of British miners discover a new way to express themselves and unexpectedly become art-world sensations. "Excitingly ambiguous, in-the-moment theater." –*NY Times.* "Heartfelt, moving and deeply politicized." –*Chicago Tribune.* [5M, 2W] ISBN: 978-0-8222-2507-2

★ **RELATIVELY SPEAKING by Ethan Coen, Elaine May and Woody Allen.** In TALKING CURE, Ethan Coen uncovers the sort of insanity that can only come from family. Elaine May explores the hilarity of passing in GEORGE IS DEAD. In HONEYMOON MOTEL, Woody Allen invites you to the sort of wedding day you won't forget. "Firecracker funny." –*NY Times.* "A rollicking good time." –*New Yorker.* [8M, 7W] ISBN: 978-0-8222-2394-8

★ **SONS OF THE PROPHET by Stephen Karam.** If to live is to suffer, then Joseph Douaihy is more alive than most. With unexplained chronic pain and the fate of his reeling family on his shoulders, Joseph's health, sanity, and insurance premium are on the line. "Explosively funny." –*NY Times.* "At once deep, deft and beautifully made." –*New Yorker.* [5M, 3W] ISBN: 978-0-8222-2597-3

★ **THE MOUNTAINTOP by Katori Hall.** A gripping reimagination of events the night before the assassination of the civil rights leader Dr. Martin Luther King, Jr. "An ominous electricity crackles through the opening moments." –*NY Times.* "[A] thrilling, wild, provocative flight of magical realism." –*Associated Press.* "Crackles with theatricality and a humanity more moving than sainthood." –*NY Newsday.* [1M, 1W] ISBN: 978-0-8222-2603-1

★ **ALL NEW PEOPLE by Zach Braff.** Charlie is 35, heartbroken, and just wants some time away from the rest of the world. Long Beach Island seems to be the perfect escape until his solitude is interrupted by a motley parade of misfits who show up and change his plans. "Consistently and sometimes sensationally funny." –*NY Times.* "A morbidly funny play about the trendy new existential condition of being young, adorable, and miserable." –*Variety.* [2M, 2W] ISBN: 978-0-8222-2562-1

NEW PLAYS

★ **CLYBOURNE PARK by Bruce Norris.** WINNER OF THE 2011 PULITZER PRIZE AND 2012 TONY AWARD. Act One takes place in 1959 as community leaders try to stop the sale of a home to a black family. Act Two is set in the same house in the present day as the now predominantly African-American neighborhood battles to hold its ground. "Vital, sharp-witted and ferociously smart." *–NY Times.* "A theatrical treasure…Indisputably, uproariously funny." *–Entertainment Weekly.* [4M, 3W] ISBN: 978-0-8222-2697-0

★ **WATER BY THE SPOONFUL by Quiara Alegría Hudes.** WINNER OF THE 2012 PULITZER PRIZE. A Puerto Rican veteran is surrounded by the North Philadelphia demons he tried to escape in the service. "This is a very funny, warm, and yes uplifting play." *–Hartford Courant.* "The play is a combination poem, prayer and app on how to cope in an age of uncertainty, speed and chaos." *–Variety.* [4M, 3W] ISBN: 978-0-8222-2716-8

★ **RED by John Logan.** WINNER OF THE 2010 TONY AWARD. Mark Rothko has just landed the biggest commission in the history of modern art. But when his young assistant, Ken, gains the confidence to challenge him, Rothko faces the agonizing possibility that his crowning achievement could also become his undoing. "Intense and exciting." *–NY Times.* "Smart, eloquent entertainment." *–New Yorker.* [2M] ISBN: 978-0-8222-2483-9

★ **VENUS IN FUR by David Ives.** Thomas, a beleaguered playwright/director, is desperate to find an actress to play Vanda, the female lead in his adaptation of the classic sadomasochistic tale *Venus in Fur*. "Ninety minutes of good, kinky fun." *–NY Times.* "A fast-paced journey into one man's entrapment by a clever, vengeful female." *–Associated Press.* [1M, 1W] ISBN: 978-0-8222-2603-1

★ **OTHER DESERT CITIES by Jon Robin Baitz.** Brooke returns home to Palm Springs after a six-year absence and announces that she is about to publish a memoir dredging up a pivotal and tragic event in the family's history—a wound they don't want reopened. "Leaves you feeling both moved and gratifyingly sated." *–NY Times.* "A genuine pleasure." *–NY Post.* [2M, 3W] ISBN: 978-0-8222-2605-5

★ **TRIBES by Nina Raine.** Billy was born deaf into a hearing family and adapts brilliantly to his family's unconventional ways, but it's not until he meets Sylvia, a young woman on the brink of deafness, that he finally understands what it means to be understood. "A smart, lively play." *–NY Times.* "[A] bright and boldly provocative drama." *–Associated Press.* [3M, 2W] ISBN: 978-0-8222-2751-9